D1177345

The Blessing of Little Girls

Sugar, Spice, & Everything Nice

PAINTINGS BY

Sandra Kuck

SWEET RIVER
PRESS
EUGENE, OREGON

The Blessing of Little Girls

Text Copyright © 2001 by Harvest House Publishers
Published by SweetRiver Press
Eugene, Oregon 97402

ISBN 1-59681-001-7

All works of art reproduced in this book are copyrighted by Sandra Kuck and may not be reproduced without the artist's permission. For more information regarding art prints featured in this book, please contact:

V.F. Fine Arts, Inc.
1737 Stibbens St. #240B
Houston, TX 77043
1.800.648.0405

Design and production by Garborg Design Works, Minneapolis, Minnesota

Harvest House Publishers has made every effort to trace the ownership of all poems and quotes. In the event of a question arising from the use of a poem or quote, we regret any error made and will be pleased to make the necessary correction in future editions of this book.

"Why God Made Little Girls" Copyright © by Art E Knight. Used by permission.

Scripture quotations are taken from The Living Bible, Copyright © 1971 owned by assignment by Illinois Bank N.A. (as trustee). Used by permission of Tyndale House Publishers, Inc., Wheaton, Illinois 60189. All rights reserved.

All rights reserved. No portion of this book may be reproduced, stored in a retrieval system, or transmitted in any form or by any means—electronic, mechanical, digital, photocopy, recording, or any other—except for brief quotations in printed reviews, without the prior permission of the publisher.

Printed in China

04 05 06 07 08 / IM / 5 4 3 2 1

Who would ever think that so much can go on in the soul of a young girl?

ANNE FRANK

3

What are little girls made of?

Sugar and spice,

And everything nice,

That's what little girls are made of.

TRADITIONAL NURSERY RHYME

5

The

knowingness

of little girls

Is hidden

underneath

their curls.

PHYLLIS McGINLEY

This girl, who was also known as Esther, was lovely in form and features, and Mordecai had taken her as his own daughter when her father and mother died.

THE BOOK OF ESTHER

$\mathcal{E}$xcuse me—I don't want to be inquisitive—but

should I be right in thinking that you are a Daughter of Eve?"

"My name is Lucy," said she, not quite understanding him.

"But you are—forgive me—you are what they call a girl?"

asked the Faun.

"Of course I'm a girl," said Lucy.

"You are in fact Human?"

"Of course I'm human," said Lucy, still a little puzzled.

C.S. LEWIS
The Lion, the Witch and the Wardrobe

What Is A Girl?

LITTLE GIRLS are the nicest things that can happen to people. They are born with a bit of angelshine about them, and though it wears thin sometimes, there is always enough left to lasso your heart—even when they are sitting in the mud, or crying temperamental tears, or parading up the street in Mother's best clothes.

A little girl can be sweeter (and badder) oftener than anyone else in the world. She can jitter around, and stomp, and make funny noises that frazzle your nerves, yet just when you open your mouth, she stands there demure with that special look in her eyes. A girl is Innocence playing in the mud, Beauty standing on its head, and Motherhood dragging a doll by the foot...

God borrows from many creatures to make a little girl. He uses the song of a bird, the squeal of a pig, the stubbornness of a mule, the antics of a monkey, the spryness of a grasshopper, the curiosity of a cat, the speed of a gazelle, the slyness of a fox, the softness of a kitten, and to top it all off He adds the mysterious mind of a woman.

A little girl likes new shoes, party dresses, small animals, first grade, noisemakers, the girl next door, dolls, make-believe, dancing lessons, ice cream, kitchens, coloring books, makeup, cans of water, going visiting, tea parties, and one boy. She doesn't care so much for visitors, boys in general, large dogs, hand-me-downs, straight chairs, vegetables, snowsuits, or staying in the front yard. She is loudest when you are thinking, the prettiest when she has provoked you, the busiest at bedtime, the quietest when you want to show her off, and the most flirtatious when she absolutely must not get the best of you again.

Who else can cause you more grief, joy, irritation, satisfaction, embarrassment, and genuine delight than this combination of Eve, Salome, and Florence Nightingale? She can muss up your home, your hair, and your dignity—spend your money, your time, and your patience—and just when your temper is ready to crack, her sunshine peeks through and you've lost again. Yes, she is a nerve-wracking nuisance, just a noisy bundle of mischief. But when your dreams tumble down and the world is a mess—when it seems you are pretty much of a fool after all—she can make you a king when she climbs on your knee and whispers, "I love you best of all!"

ALAN BECK

DADDY'S *Little* *Girl*

A little girl brought a gift to her father and said, "This is for you, Daddy." He looked at her in confusion when he found the box empty. "Don't you know that when you give someone a present, there's supposed to be something inside it?"

The little girl looked up at him and said, "Oh, Daddy, it is not empty. I blew kisses into the box. All for you, Daddy."

AUTHOR UNKNOWN

God made the world with its towering trees

Majestic mountains and restless seas

Then paused and said, "It needs one more thing...

Someone to laugh and dance and sing

To walk in the woods and gather flowers

To commune with nature in quiet hours."

Why God Made Little Girls

So God made little girls

With laughing eyes and bouncing curls

With joyful hearts and infectious smiles

Enchanting ways and feminine wiles

And when He'd completed the task He'd begun

He was pleased and proud of the job He'd done

For the world, when seen through a little girl's eyes

Greatly resembles paradise.

ARTHUR E. KNIGHT

Little

girls

are . . .

A sweet new blossom of humanity,

fresh fallen from God's own home,

to flower on earth.

WILLIAM MASSEY

A toddling little girl is a center of

common feeling which makes the most

dissimilar people understand each other.

GEORGE ELIOT

La, child! you needn't mind that. I'll take care of you, and fix you up, so you won't look odd."

"Am I odd?" asked Polly, struck by the word, and hoping it didn't mean anything very bad.

"You are a dear, and ever so much prettier than you were last summer,

Often God's biggest gifts to us come i

only you've been brought up different-
ly from us; so your ways are not like
ours, you see," began Fanny,
finding it rather hard to explain.

"How different?" asked Polly again,
for she liked to understand things.

"Well, you dress like a little girl,
for one thing."

"I *am* a little girl; so why shouldn't
I?" and Polly looked at her simple
blue merino frock, stout boots, and
short hair, with a puzzled air.

"You are fourteen; and *we* consid-
er ourselves young ladies at that age,"
continued Fanny, surveying, with

complacency, the pile of hair on the
top of her head, with a fringe of fuzz
'round her forehead, and a wavy lock
streaming down her back; likewise her
scarlet-and-black suit, with its big
sash, little *pannier*, bright buttons,
points, rosettes—and, heaven knows
what. There was a locket on her neck,
ear-rings tinkling in her ears, watch
and chain at her belt, and several rings
on a pair of hands that would have
been improved by soap and water.

LOUISA MAY ALCOTT
An Old-Fashioned Girl

he littlest of packages...our children.
ANONYMOUS

I hear in the chamber above me

The patter of little feet

The sound of a door that is open,

And voices soft and sweet.

From my study I see in the lamplight

Descending the broad hall stair,

Grave Alice, and laughing Allegra,

And Edith with golden hair.

A whisper, and then a silence:

Yet I know by the merry eyes

They are plotting and planning together

To take me by surprise.

HENRY WADSWORTH LONGFELLOW

Yes, and do you know why the stars are so full of joy, and wink at us so with their eyes?" asked Heidi.

"No, I don't know; what do you think about it?" asked Klara.

"Because they see up in heaven how well the dear Lord directs everything for people, so that they need have no anxiety and can be safe, because everything will happen for the best. That delights them so; see how they wink, that we may be happy too! But do you know, Klara, we must not forget our prayers; we must ask the dear Lord to think of us, when he is directing everything so well, that we may always be safe and never be afraid of anything."

So the children sat up in bed and said their evening prayer. Then Heidi laid her head on her round arm and was asleep in a moment. But Klara stayed awake for a long time, for she had never seen anything so wonderful in her life as this sleeping room in the starlight.

Johanna Spyri
Heidi

23

Polly had learned this secret. She loved to do the "little things" that others did not see, or were too busy to stop for; and while doing them, without a thought of thanks, she made sunshine for herself as well as others. There was so much love in her own home, that she quickly felt the want of it in Fanny's, and puzzled herself to find out why these people were not kind and patient to one another. She did not try to settle the question, but did her best to love and serve and bear with each; and the goodwill, the gentle heart, the helpful ways and simple manners of our Polly made her dear to everyone, for these virtues, even in a little child, are lovely and attractive.

LOUISA MAY ALCOTT
An Old-Fashioned Girl

LITTLE GIRLIE, KNEELING THERE,

LISPING LOW YOUR EVENING PRAYER,

ASKING GOD ABOVE TO BLESS ME

AT THE CLOSING OF EACH DAY,

OFT THE TEARS COME TO MY EYES,

AND I FEEL A BIG LUMP RISE

IN MY THROAT, THAT I CAN'T SWALLOW,

AND I SOMETIMES TURN AWAY.

EDGAR GUEST

Three little maids from school are we,

Pert as a schoolgirl well can be,

Filled to the brim with girlish glee.

W.S. GILBERT

There was a little girl

Who had a little curl

Right in the middle of her forehead.

When she was good

She was very, very good

But when she was bad she was horrid.

HENRY WADSWORTH LONGFELLOW

Little Girls

God made the little boys for fun, for rough and tumble times of play;

He made their little legs to run and race and scamper through the day.

He made them strong for climbing trees, he suited them for horns and drums,

And filled them full of revelries, so they could be their father's chums.

But then He saw that gentle ways must also travel from above.

And so, through all our troubled days He sent us little girls to love.

He knew that earth would never do, unless a bit of Heaven it had.

Men needed eyes divinely blue to toil by day and still be glad.

A world where only men and boys made merry would in time grow stale,

And so He shared His Heavenly joys that faith in Him should never fail.

He sent us down a thousand charms, He decked our ways with golden curls

And laughing eyes and dimpled arms. He let us have His little girls.

They are the tenderest of His flowers, the little angels of His flock,

And we may keep and call them ours, until God's messenger shall knock.

They bring to us the gentleness and beauty that we sorely need;

They soothe us with each fond caress and strengthen us for every deed.

And happy should that mortal be whom God has trusted through the years,

To guard a little girl and see that she is kept from pain and tears.

EDGAR GUEST

Come along in then, little girl!

Or else stay out!

But in the open door she stands,

And bites her lip and twists her hands,

And stares upon me, trouble-eyed;

"Mother," she says, "I can't decide!"

EDNA ST. VINCENT MILLAY

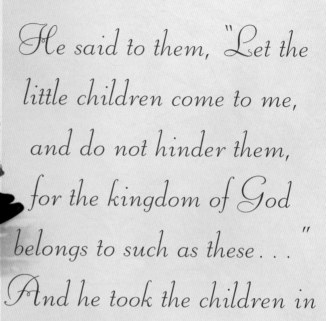

He said to them, "Let the
little children come to me,
and do not hinder them,
for the kingdom of God
belongs to such as these . . ."
And he took the children in
his arms, put his hands on
them and blessed them.

—❧—

THE BOOK OF MARK

A Child to Love

You can have your wealth and riches,

All the things so many seek,

Position, power, and success,

The fame you long to keep.

You can earn as much as you wish,

Reach a status high above,

But none of these can equal

Having one sweet child to love.

'Tis the greatest gift from heaven,

Little arms that hold you tight,

And a kiss so soft and gentle

When you tuck them in at night.

A million precious questions

And each story often read,

Two eyes so bright and smiling,

And a darling tousled head.

God has never matched the goodness

Of a trusting little face,

Or a heart so full of laughter

Spreading sunshine every place.

A child to hold and cuddle,

'Tis a gift from God above,

And the world is so much brighter

When you have a child to love.

Author Unknown

$\mathcal{A}$my, though the youngest, was a most important person—in her own opinion at least. A regular snow-maiden, with blue eyes, and yellow hair, curling on her shoulders, pale and slender, and always carrying herself like a young lady mindful of her manners.

Louisa May Alcott
Little Women

Sandra Kuck
©1999

39

What the frog said, happened, and the queen had a little girl that was so beautiful that the king could not contain himself for joy, and made a great feast. He invited not only his relatives, friends, and acquaintances, but also the wise women, that they might be gracious and kind to the child…The feast was splendidly celebrated, and when it was over the wise women gave the child their wonderful gifts. One gave her virtue, another beauty, another wealth, and so with everything that people want in the world.

THE BROTHERS GRIMM
Sleeping Beauty

DON'T LET ANYONE THINK LITTLE OF YOU BECAUSE YOU ARE YOUNG. BE THEIR IDEAL…BE A PATTERN FOR THEM IN YOUR LOVE, YOUR FAITH, AND YOUR CLEAN THOUGHTS.

THE BOOK OF I TIMOTHY

ADVICE TO
Little Girls

Good little girls ought not to make mouths at their teachers for every trifling offence. This retaliation should only be resorted to under peculiarly aggravated circumstances.

If at any time you find it necessary to correct your brother, do not correct him with mud—never, on any account, throw mud at him, because it will spoil his clothes. It is better to scold him a little, for then you obtain desirable results. You secure his immediate attention to the lessons you are inculcating, and at the same time your hot water will have a tendency to move impurities from his person, and possibly the skin, in spots.

If your mother tells you to do a thing, it is wrong to reply that you won't. It is better and more becoming to intimate that you will do as she bids you, and then afterwards act quietly in the matter according to the dictates of your best judgment.

Good little girls always show marked deference for the aged. You ought never to "sass" old people unless they "sass" you first.

MARK TWAIN

43

Mary, Mary, quite contrary,

How does your garden grow?

With silver bells and cockle shells,

And pretty maids in a row.

TRADITIONAL NURSERY RHYME

"Yes, I dote on Miss Georgiana!" cried the fervent Abbot. "Little darling!—with her long curls and her blue eyes, and such a sweet colour as she has; just as if she were painted!"

CHARLOTTE BRONTË
Jane Eyre

45

"A remarkable child," said one of the sailors as Pippi
disappeared in the distance.

He was right. Pippi was indeed a remarkable child.
The most remarkable thing about her was that she was
so strong. She was so very strong that in the whole wide
world there was not a single police officer who was as strong
as she. Why, she could lift a whole horse if she wanted to!

ASTRID LINDGREN
Pippi Longstocking

Pink bows and pretty things,
Fancy dresses and golden rings,
Little girl wishes and princess dreams,
She dances on stars and moonlight beams.

VERONICA CURTIS